# FAST
# FLOWER
# ARRANGING

# FAST
# FLOWER
# ARRANGING

# JANE PACKER

DK PUBLISHING, INC.

# A DK PUBLISHING BOOK

**Project Editor**
Annabel Kantaria

**Art Editor**
Emy Manby

**Senior Art Editor**
Tracey Clarke

**US Editor**
Ray Rogers

**Managing Editors**
Susannah Marriott, Mary Ling

**Managing Art Editor**
Toni Kay

**DTP Designer**
Karen Ruane

**Production Manager**
Maryann Webster

**Photography**
Dave King

*For Gary, Rebs, Lola, and Ted*

First American edition, 1998
2 4 6 8 10 9 7 5 3 1
Published in the United States by
DK Publishing Inc.,
95 Madison Avenue, New York, New York 10016

Library of Congress Cataloging-in-Publication Data
Packer, Jane, 1959-
    Fast flower arranging / by Jane Packer. – 1st American ed.
        p.    cm.
    Includes index.
    ISBN 0-7894-2394-4
    1. Flower arrangement.    2. Flowers.    I. Title.
SB449.P2218    1998
745.92–dc21                                    97–38653
                                                    CIP

Reproduced in Italy by GRB Editrice, Verona
Printed and bound in Italy

# CONTENTS

# INTRODUCTION

THIS BOOK IS FOR the thousands of people who every so often buy a bunch of flowers as they tear around the supermarket, rush home after a busy day, or suddenly feel inspired to visit their local florist. In other words, this book is not necessarily aimed at flower arrangers (in fact, mention the words "flower arranging" to many, and they will beat a hasty retreat). My ideas are for those who simply love flowers but who perhaps don't have the time or inclination to plan and create the formal displays so beloved by ardent floral experts.

Not everyone wants to spend hours designing elaborate masterpieces (few of us have the time), but, with a little help, that bunch of flowers you have brought home and placed gingerly in the nearest vase can be transformed into an eye-catching arrangement.

This book will demonstrate that a few fast ideas are all you need to be able to present your flowers successfully and with the minimum amount of fuss. Today's flower fashion is instant and spontaneous. It is a new look that suits modern lifestyles, and it bears scant resemblance to the complicated flower fantasies that are often available from designer florists.

Flowers should not be the preserve of specialists: their fragrance and color lift every setting, and a simple, unconstrained display of flowers can evoke a sense of calm, create a mood of indulgence, and even seem to enhance our quality of life. The fast ideas that fill this book prove that all you need is a love of flowers and a little imagination to create a look that perfectly suits your modern lifestyle – enjoy!

Jane Packer

# A GALLERY OF FLOWERS

THE GALLERY OF FLOWERS SHOWS JUST A FRACTION OF THE VAST

SPECTRUM OF VARIETIES AVAILABLE. SOMETIMES

THE COLOR AND SHAPE OF A FLOWER IS

IMPORTANT FOR YOUR CHOSEN

LOOK, YET ONLY AN EXPERT

SUPPLIER COULD MATCH YOUR

DESCRIPTION TO A PARTICULAR

VARIETY. HOWEVER, THIS DELIGHTFUL

SELECTION WILL PROVIDE YOU WITH A RICH

STARTER PALETTE OF COLORS, SHAPES, AND

FRAGRANCES TO HELP YOU PLAN YOUR DISPLAYS.

# DAFFODILS

THESE CHEERFUL SPRING FLOWERS can be identified by the

characteristic trumpet or cup surrounded by a ring of six petals.

Daffodils bloom in shades of white and yellow to orange and

red. They are usually bought without their foliage: expose

long, straight stems as the deliberate focal point of

a display. Mass daffodils together for a sunny spot

of color, or mix them with other flowers

for a bright splash of spring.

KEY FACTS
.............................................

AVAILABILITY: Winter to spring
FRAGRANCE: ❀ ❀
LIFESPAN: 🏺 🏺
.............................................

**See also:** Daffodil Topiary Tree 38; Instant Effects with Daffodils 40.

# HYACINTHS & FREESIAS

THE HEAVILY PERFUMED HYACINTH'S dense spike of glossy

flowers comes in shades of blue, pink, white, and, more

unusually, shades of apricot. Popular for wired bridal

work, this spring bulb can also be used in pots

or in cut-flower arrangements. The

trumpet-shaped freesia lasts well, and its

fresh colors and heady scent make it a

favorite at weddings, too. Mix and match

bright shades or opt for the striking

look of a single-color bunch for

an extra-special, fast display.

### KEY FACTS: HYACINTHS

AVAILABILITY: Autumn to spring
FRAGRANCE: ✿ ✿ ✿
LIFESPAN: ⚘ ⚘ ⚘

### KEY FACTS: FREESIAS

AVAILABILITY: All year
FRAGRANCE: ✿ ✿ ✿
LIFESPAN: ⚘ ⚘

See also: Hanging Freesias 42; Hyacinth Centerpiece 44; Hyacinth Displays 46.

# TULIPS

EVER GRACEFUL AND HUGELY VERSATILE, tulips are cultivated in a rich variety of colors, shapes, and sizes. More unusual examples include ornate parrot tulips with serrated edges, and double blooms with extra layers of petals. When using tulips in formal arrangements, be aware that once placed in water, most varieties will grow about 2in (5cm), and the heads will bend toward the light. Always look for a strong, firm leaf as a sign of quality.

## KEY FACTS

AVAILABILITY: Winter to spring

FRAGRANCE: ❀

LIFESPAN: 🌷 🌷

See also: Tulips in Raffia 48; Instant Effects with Tulips 50.

# RANUNCULUS

WITH THEIR DENSE TIERS OF PETALS, these opulent flowers

are reminiscent of ladies' ball gowns, looking their best

when open and "full-skirted": sometimes the fragile stems

look as if they cannot support the weight of the petals.

The wide variety of colors available makes

ranunculus versatile: en masse

they can look very modern;

mixed with other flowers

in a rustic jug they take on

a charming, cottagey look.

### KEY FACTS

AVAILABILITY: Spring

FRAGRANCE: 🌸

LIFESPAN: 🌷🌷

See also: White Ranunculus 52; Ranunculus Displays 54.

# PEONIES

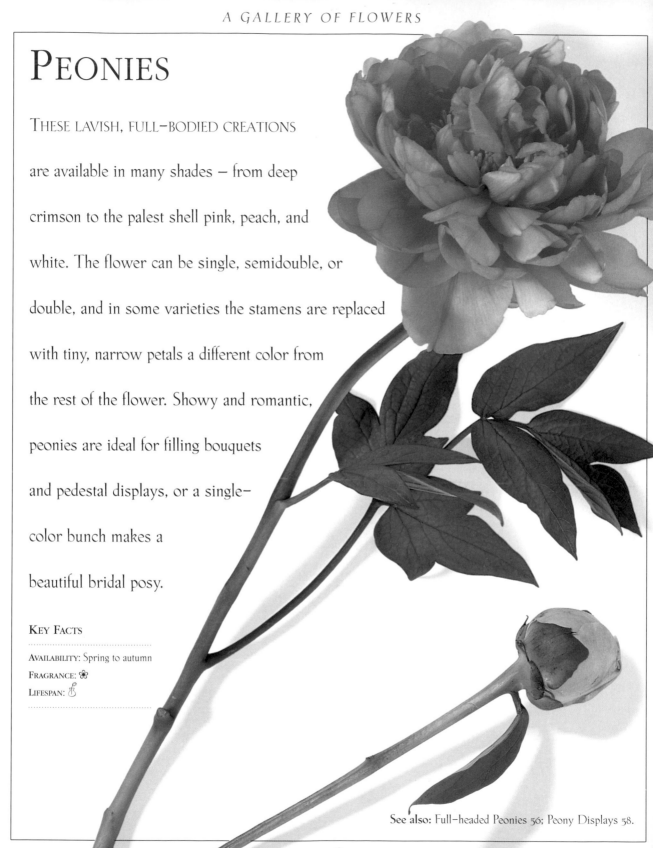

THESE LAVISH, FULL-BODIED CREATIONS
are available in many shades – from deep
crimson to the palest shell pink, peach, and
white. The flower can be single, semidouble, or
double, and in some varieties the stamens are replaced
with tiny, narrow petals a different color from
the rest of the flower. Showy and romantic,
peonies are ideal for filling bouquets
and pedestal displays, or a single-
color bunch makes a
beautiful bridal posy.

KEY FACTS

AVAILABILITY: Spring to autumn
FRAGRANCE: ❀
LIFESPAN: ⚱

**See also:** Full-headed Peonies 56; Peony Displays 58.

# ROSES

THERE ARE LITERALLY THOUSANDS OF VARIETIES

of rose. Flowers can be double, cupped, rounded,

or rosette-shaped and range from miniatures

the size of a fingernail to old-fashioned garden

roses as big as a salad plate. The

ever-increasing popularity of the

rose means that new varieties are

constantly appearing, with growers

making efforts to improve lifespan,

scent, and color.

### KEY FACTS

AVAILABILITY: All year
FRAGRANCE: None to 🌸🌸🌸
LIFESPAN: 🌹🌹

See also: Tins of Roses 60; Instant Effects with Roses 62.

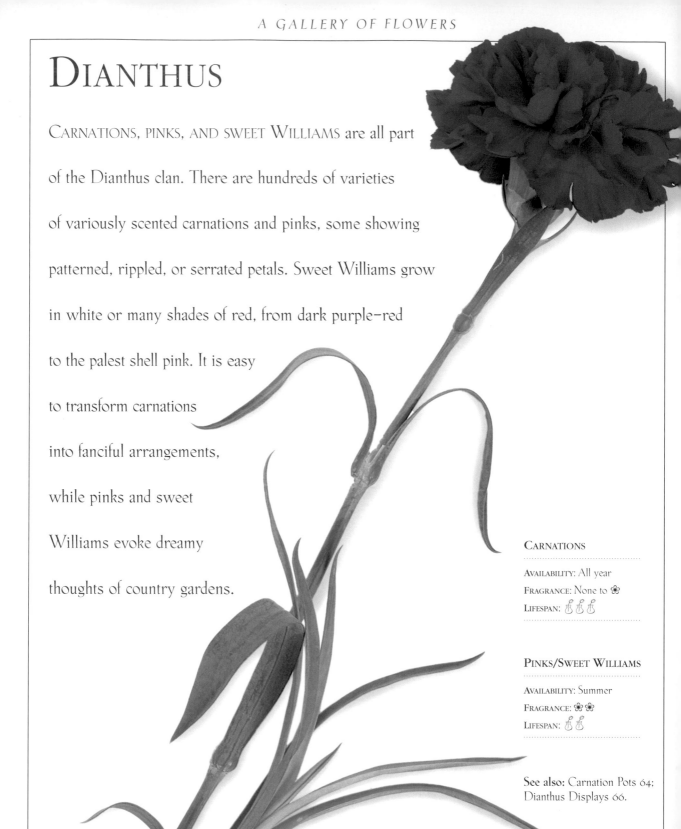

# DIANTHUS

CARNATIONS, PINKS, AND SWEET WILLIAMS are all part

of the Dianthus clan. There are hundreds of varieties

of variously scented carnations and pinks, some showing

patterned, rippled, or serrated petals. Sweet Williams grow

in white or many shades of red, from dark purple-red

to the palest shell pink. It is easy

to transform carnations

into fanciful arrangements,

while pinks and sweet

Williams evoke dreamy

thoughts of country gardens.

**CARNATIONS**

AVAILABILITY: All year

FRAGRANCE: None to ✿

LIFESPAN: 🌱🌱🌱

**PINKS/SWEET WILLIAMS**

AVAILABILITY: Summer

FRAGRANCE: ✿✿

LIFESPAN: 🌱🌱

**See also:** Carnation Pots 64;
Dianthus Displays 66.

# SUNFLOWERS

NAMED FOR THEIR GLORIOUS YELLOW FLOWERS,

these floral giants are the epitome of hot summer days.

As cut flowers, however, they are available nearly all year,

and breeding has led to a range of novel characteristics

such as miniature heads, double rings of petals,

yellow centers, and even amber petals.

KEY FACTS
.....................................................
AVAILABILITY: Nearly all year
FRAGRANCE: ✿
LIFESPAN: ♣
.....................................................

**See also:** Modern Sunflowers 68; Sunflower Displays 70.

# DAHLIAS

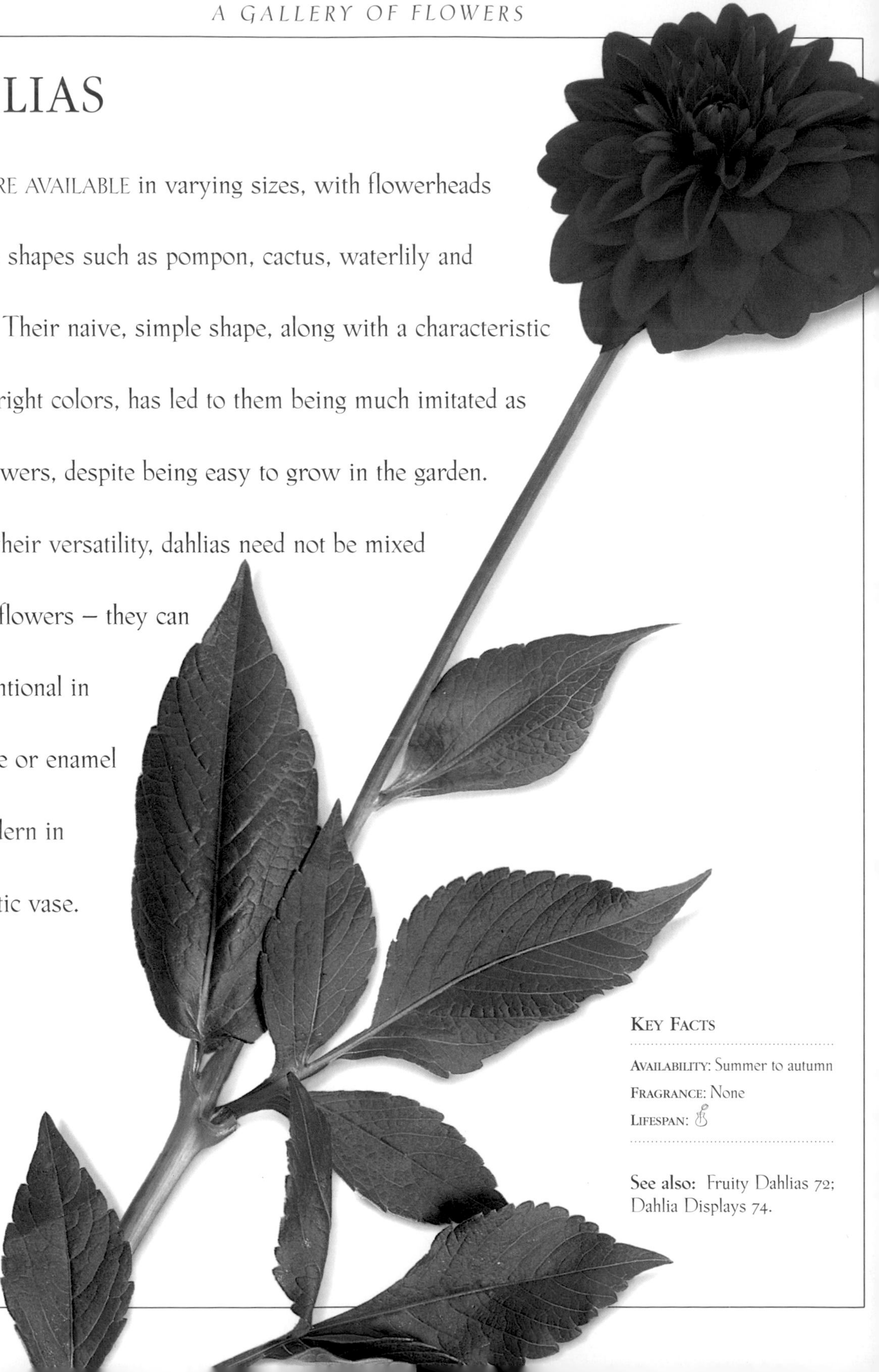

DAHLIAS ARE AVAILABLE in varying sizes, with flowerheads

that include shapes such as pompon, cactus, waterlily and

decorative. Their naive, simple shape, along with a characteristic

palette of bright colors, has led to them being much imitated as

artificial flowers, despite being easy to grow in the garden.

Thanks to their versatility, dahlias need not be mixed

with other flowers – they can

look conventional in

a stoneware or enamel

jug, or modern in

a zany plastic vase.

## KEY FACTS

AVAILABILITY: Summer to autumn
FRAGRANCE: None
LIFESPAN: 

See also:  Fruity Dahlias 72;
Dahlia Displays 74.

# LILIES

EXOTIC-LOOKING, SHOWY, COLORFUL, and often
fragrant, lilies are an excellent choice for cut-flower
displays. The white lily has a supreme grace that
makes it a favorite on special occasions.

Flowers are bowl-, funnel-,

Turk's cap-, or trumpet-shaped,

with petals sometimes striped

or dotted. Some florists

remove the stamens,

which can make

stubborn pollen

stains on fabric.

**KEY FACTS**

AVAILABILITY: All year

FRAGRANCE: None to ✿ ✿ ✿

LIFESPAN: 🎺 🎺 🎺

**See also:** Oriental Lilies 76; Lily Displays 78.

# GERBERAS

THESE POPULAR, DAISYLIKE FLOWERS are cultivated in an

ever-increasing array of varieties including single, double,

and fancy flowerheads. Colors range from very pale to

bright and zingy. The simple shape of the flower

always seems modern and perhaps even

architectural, allowing a single stem

to steal the show in a clear glass

vase. A few well-chosen

blooms can update a more

traditional arrangement.

## KEY FACTS

AVAILABILITY: All year

FRAGRANCE: None

LIFESPAN:

**See also:** Inside-out Gerberas 80; Instant Effects with Gerberas 82.

# FRUITS & VEGETABLES

MANY ORDINARY FRUITS AND VEGETABLES make welcome additions to flower arrangements.

Although you can experiment with exotic items, the effects can be just as dramatic using

more easily obtainable ones. Color counts, of course, when choosing produce, but the

most noticeable feature is often the skin – look for unusual texture or a radiant sheen.

**CABBAGE-LEAF VASE**
Tie cabbage leaves around a
vase and fill with vegetables
and flowers that pick out the
wintry purple tones.

See also: Fruity Dahlias 72;
Watermelon Vase 84.

RED APPLE

BLACK GRAPES

MINIATURE
PINEAPPLE

ZUCCHINI

EGGPLANTS

SCALLIONS

RED ONION

CHILIES

RADICCHIO

# FOLIAGE

THE IMPORTANCE OF FOLIAGE in an arrangement should not be underestimated – the shape, color, and texture of the leaves can drastically alter the appearance of the flowers. For example, stiff, upright, glossy foliage will make a rose look exclusive and elegant, but trailing foliage will make it appear more soft and feminine. Where possible, try to use seasonal foliage to complement seasonal flowers.

HYPERICUM

See also: Ivy Wreaths 86.

BUTCHER'S BROOM

BOXWOOD

LEATHERLEAF

SPRING CATKINS

BERRIED IVY

LAURUSTINUS

HOLLY

ENGLISH IVY

EUCALYPTUS

# FIVE-MINUTE DISPLAYS

THIS SECTION SHOWS HOW TO ACHIEVE A POLISHED, COHESIVE LOOK IN A

MATTER OF MINUTES: ALTHOUGH SOME OF THE DISPLAYS MAY TAKE A LITTLE

LONGER, THEY ARE WORTH THE EXTRA EFFORT. DON'T FEEL BOUND

TO COPY THESE IDEAS EXACTLY. INSTEAD, USE THEM

AS A SPRINGBOARD FOR YOUR OWN CREATIVE

COMBINATIONS, AND REMEMBER TO CHOOSE

THE CONTAINER WITH CARE: SHAPE, SIZE, AND

COLOR ALL INFLUENCE THE END RESULT.

AS I HAVE SHOWN ON THE FOLLOWING

PAGES, EVEN THE SIMPLEST DESIGN CONCEPTS

CAN HAVE TREMENDOUS VISUAL IMPACT.

# DAFFODIL TOPIARY TREE

## YOU WILL NEED

*Raffia*

*5–6 bunches of daffodils*    *Glass jar*    *Large terracotta pot*    *2 handfuls of moss*

NOTHING LOOKS FRESHER for spring than a densely packed bundle of bright yellow daffodils. Rather than displaying the flowers in a vase, I have used them to make this unusual version of a topiary tree, contrasting the signature color of the petals with a strong, dark container. The result is quirky, fun, and very easy to make, but remember to replenish the water to prolong the life of the flowers.

## MAKING THE TOPIARY TREE

To keep the trunk of the topiary tree neat, make sure that the stems do not get twisted as they are put into position.

CREATE A DOME EFFECT with the heads by adding each circle of flowers lower than the previous one

*1 Starting with one stem in your hand, add stems one by one in circles around it, positioning them so the heads lean outward. After adding the last flower, tie raffia around the bunch, just below the heads, then trim the stems.*

*2 Place the tied stems in the glass jar half-filled with water, then position the jar in the terracotta pot. Press moss around the stems at the top of the pot to finish. Replenish with water as required.*

RAFFIA tied
in a knot or bow

STANDING STEMS
Bound together, the bare,
straight stems of the
daffodils become the trunk
of the topiary tree.

MOSS fills the gap
between the stems
and the vase

# INSTANT EFFECTS WITH DAFFODILS

*YOU CAN CREATE WILDLY DIFFERENT LOOKS with the variety of daffodils available, gaining as much impact from a single stem as from a large bunch massed together. Use other foliage to prevent the long daffodil stems from looking bare, and choose a container carefully.*

## USING COLOR AND SHAPE

**INFORMAL TOPIARY**
Choose a vase to emphasize the golden color at the center of each flower.

**MASSED FLOWERS**
Contrast pale flowers with a strongly colored vase for a dynamic look.

**COUNTRY LOOK**
Use a vase in the same lime-green shade as the foliage to exaggerate its hue.

**MODERN SIMPLICITY**
Cut two varieties of blooms down short, then pack into a contrasting blue glass vase.

**COMPLEMENTARY COLORS**
Here the foliage links the flowers with the vase, softening the look of the daffodils.

**SIMPLE STEMS**
Two stems of 'Soleil d'Or' are perfect for the color and shape of this bud vase.

PLANTED DAFFODILS
Use natural accessories, such as moss, stones, and twigs, to dress up potted plants.

TWIG FENCING tied with green string links the colors of the basket and the stems

MOSS hides the potting soil

WIRE BASKET is a modern alternative to a wicker basket

# HANGING FREESIAS

## YOU WILL NEED

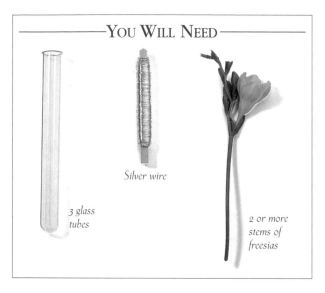

*Silver wire*

*3 glass tubes*

*2 or more stems of freesias*

THE VIBRANT AND CHEERFUL COLORS of freesias can be shown off to best advantage in the simplest displays. Here, dainty glass tubes containing a couple of stems are hung from gleaming silver wire. It is a versatile idea: you could pin a few to a corkboard to brighten up an office, hang several tubes across a window to catch the light, or tie many tubes to a tree for a novel Christmas decoration.

## MAKING THE FREESIA DISPLAY

Make sure you have enough wire to hang the tubes at the desired height.

*1* Wind the wire around the top of a glass tube to make a cuff, then twist to secure it.

*2* Fill the tube with water and place one or two freesia stems in it. To finish, pin the tube to a corkboard or hang it in a window.

FREESIAS have foliage-free stems that are ideal for this display

### PINNED FLOWERS
A few of these fragrant arrangements fastened to a corkboard are a cost-effective way to bring color to a room. Try to position them near a window to let the water and silver wire catch the light.

# HYACINTH CENTERPIECE

VERSATILE HYACINTHS are currently enjoying a revival as a fashionable flower. Change the mood of this magnificent display by experimenting with different containers: earthenware for a rustic country feel, glass for stark modernism. Here, the glass tank leaves the naked silver roots visible as they trail in the shimmering water, while the crown of deep purple bulbs makes the arrangement all the more tantalizing.

## YOU WILL NEED

Low glass tank

20 stems of hyacinth

Cylindrical glass vase

14 clean hyacinth bulbs

## MAKING THE CENTERPIECE

Rest the bulbs on the edge of the glass tank, just above the water level. The cut flowers will last up to 10 days, but change the water every 2–3 days.

**1** *Fill the vase with water and place it in the center of the tank. Half-fill the tank with water. Working from the outside in, arrange the cut hyacinths in the vase, slanting the stems neatly.*

**2** *Place the bulbs one by one in a ring around the inner vase. Rest them on the rim of the tank so the roots touch the water, but make sure the bulbs themselves stay out of the water.*

**ADAPTABLE DISPLAY**
When the cut flowers in the center begin to wilt, remove them and fill the vase with pebbles.

# HYACINTH DISPLAYS

THE EARTHY TONES of terracotta pots are the perfect foil for the vibrant greens, pinks, and blues of these hyacinths. A glass container filled with pebbles and shells creates a completely different look, while the loosely wrapped flowers would make a perfect simple gift.

**CUT FLOWERS**
Pay attention to the color of the container: here, shocking pink and electric blue make the most of two simple arrangements.

**BRIGHT TISSUE PAPER**
tied with green string envelops a bunch of blue flowers

**BLUE GLASS TUMBLER**
gives easy charm to two stems of hyacinth

**POTTED PLANTS**
Make a refreshing change
from cut flowers by planting
hyacinth bulbs in shaped
terracotta pots. Hide the soil
with moss, and remember to
water it regularly.

A SPIKE of hyacinths
adds a fresh scent
to a room

BUDS are
about to open

MOSS
covers the
soil and
softens the
overall effect

PEBBLES AND SHELLS
surround a hyacinth
placed in a glass tank

# TULIPS IN RAFFIA

---

### YOU WILL NEED

| | | | | |
|---|---|---|---|---|
| *Large glass tank* | | | | |
| *Small glass vase* | *Bundle of raffia* | *4 edged tulips* | *6 pink tulips* | *10 purple tulips* |

---

THIS LUXURIOUS DISPLAY of tulips sits cradled in a bushy nest of raffia, dramatically changing the appearance of a plain glass tank. Although I have used raffia in a color that complements the tulips, the display would look equally stunning in clashing oranges, reds, and pinks. For a more natural look, fill the tank with pebbles, shells, wool in neutral tones, or textured tissue paper.

## MAKING THE DISPLAY

To prevent rot, remember to remove the lower leaves from the tulips before putting them in water. For a stark, modern look, remove the leaves completely.

*1 Fill the small vase with water and place it in the center of the glass tank. Push the raffia into the gap between the two containers so it completely hides the inner vase. Arrange the raffia to look attractive.*

*2 Position the purple tulips in a ring around the outer edge of the vase so their heads hang comfortably over the edge of the large tank. To finish, arrange the pink and edged tulips into a loose ring inside the purple ones.*

**NATURAL LOOK**
This charming display is
achieved by placing the tulips
loosely so they do not
appear too formal.

PINK TULIPS form a
contrasting circle in the
center of the arrangement

**OUTER TULIPS**
soften the look
by draping gently
over the edge of
the tank

RAFFIA BETWEEN
the vase and tank
hides the stems

# INSTANT EFFECTS WITH TULIPS

*WHAT COULD BE QUICKER than plunging a handful of flowers into a vase?*

*The key is to consider color and form when matching flowers to vases. Be bold,*

*whether using just a few stems or mixing a mass of blooms with foliage.*

## USING COLOR AND SHAPE

**STRONG STATEMENT**
A bold choice of a bright cerise vase
is a shocking match for pink tulips.

**SOFT PASTEL SHADES**
Enhance the tulips' lemony tinge by
blending them with a pale yellow vase.

**CONTRASTING TONES**
For a lively modern display, juxtapose
fiery orange tulips with a green vase.

**FLARED VASE**
Fill this vase with enough stems to arch
over the edge in a sweeping curve.

**NARROW-NECKED VASE**
This vase requires only a small number
of tulips to fill it attractively.

**LOW, WIDE BOWL**
Don't be afraid to cut tulips down
for a low, compact display.

TERRACOTTA VASE is filled with glossy, berried ivy and parrot tulips

NEW WAYS
WITH FOLIAGE
Break the rules by wrapping ivy leaves *around* the vase (far right). Secured with copper wire, these leaves create a welcome alternative to the ubiquitous glass cube vase. Cut tulips low, so the heads appear just above the rim.

# WHITE RANUNCULUS

THIS COOL AND AIRY DISPLAY is easy to achieve using the heavy-headed blooms of white ranunculus. Choose a vase that flares out at the top: with a large quantity of flowers the stems will drape opulently over the side. The white shells and pebbles that fill the vase are not only evocative of sunny days and sandy beaches, they complement the color of the ranunculus and help raise and support the stems.

## MAKING THE DISPLAY

Feed the ranunculus stems between the shells and pebbles. This allows you to position each stem exactly where it is needed.

*2 Place the ranunculus in the vase, working in a ring around the edge. Gently push each stem into the shells and pebbles. To finish, add stems to the center of the display.*

*1 Half-fill the vase with shells and pebbles, pulling the more attractive ones to the front. Fill the vase with water.*

FLOWERS extend
well beyond the
edge of the vase

POLISHED SHELLS
shimmer in the water

PALE AND INTERESTING
Cool whites make this the
perfect decoration for hot
summer days.

# RANUNCULUS DISPLAYS

THE NATURAL BEAUTY OF RANUNCULUS is such that I feel they need no extra adornment. As layer upon layer of voluptuous petals open, the heads appear to get heavier, making the delicate stems bend and twist, allowing the flowers to droop lazily over the edge of the container.

**PURE AND SIMPLE**
Mass white ranunculus together in small aluminum pots, then place them on a silver tray around a four-wick candle.

**BUDS** provide color contrast

**FIERY BRIGHT**
Start by positioning the flowers around the edge of the container, then build them up toward the center, resting them on each other. The display would also work with blooms such as marigolds or asters.

TOPIARY TREE
of pink ranunculus
(see page 58)

GLASS TUBES
draw attention to
the beautiful stems

RANUNCULUS are cut
down low and mixed
with pink snowberries

# FULL-HEADED PEONIES

LUSCIOUS PEONIES, familiar as country garden flowers, take on a contemporary look when a single-color bunch is placed in a brightly colored vase. Although the display looks very natural, the heavy-headed blooms are held in position with a grid of tape, while the flared neck of the vase makes it possible to create a full display without using a huge number of flowers.

## MAKING THE DISPLAY

Leave the stems in the center of the arrangement slightly longer than the outside ones to create a domed effect, or cut them all to the same height for a flat-topped display.

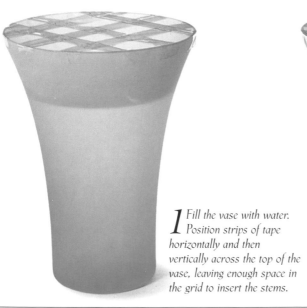

*1 Fill the vase with water. Position strips of tape horizontally and then vertically across the top of the vase, leaving enough space in the grid to insert the stems.*

*2 Starting at the outside, place one peony in each small corner hole of the grid, and two in each of the larger holes. Position them so the foliage surrounds the flowers.*

**CENTRAL BLOOMS** are
held in place by a tape grid

**YELLOW STAMENS**
provide a delightful
color contrast

**OUTER RING** of foliage
hides any visible tape and
frames the flowers

**FROSTED GREEN GLASS**
vase gives the peonies
a modern feel

**MONOCHROME**
Flowers in shades of the
same color sometimes
make more of an impact
than a mixed bouquet.

# PEONY DISPLAYS

THE LUSH OPULENCE OF PEONIES, their huge heads crammed with masses of petals, makes them one of my favorite flowers. Ideally suited to an old-fashioned country look when mixed with foliage and placed in a pitcher, peonies can also look clean and stylish in a contemporary glass vase.

**RED CHERRIES**
Position a tumbler of water in the center of the tank, then surround it with cherries. Fill the tumbler with peonies and roses.

ZEBRA ROSES work beautifully with the peonies, adding extra shades of pink

STEMS CUT TO DIFFERENT
heights create a natural look

COUNTRY GARDEN PITCHERS
To ensure your arrangement
does not look too contrived or
formal, group about five stems
of each flower together within
the display.

SPIKES OF PINK ASTILBE
blend with the pink peonies

LIME GREEN lady's
mantle adds vibrancy
to the deep pink of
the peonies

ASTILBE FOLIAGE
frames the flowers

# TINS OF ROSES

THIS CONTEMPORARY DISPLAY of roses plays with striking contrasts of color and texture. The flowers are packed into square blocks of solid color, and any foliage that might interrupt the effect is stripped away. Cutting the stems short prolongs the life of the roses, since water reaches the heads more easily. The look could also be achieved with other bold flowers such as tulips, anemones, carnations, or asters.

## MAKING THE DISPLAY

Make sure the roses are exactly the same height. If they differ even slightly, the impact of the blocks of color will be lost.

*1 Using one tin as a measure, cut the stem of the first rose at a sharp diagonal, so the head sits just above the rim. Cut the rest of the roses to the same height. Fill the tins with water.*

*2 Line the edges of the tin with the tighter buds, then use the more open flowers to fill the center. Repeat this process using a single color of rose in each tin. Arrange the tins.*

**CHECKERED BED**
Making four tins gives you
the flexibility to try different
arrangements: line the tins
up for a windowsill display,
or push them together to
make a stunning focal point.

TIN CONTAINERS
contrast with the soft
ruffles of the flowers

FLOWERS support
each other

# INSTANT EFFECTS WITH ROSES

*INCREDIBLY VERSATILE and usually scented, roses have a fantastic ability to take on many different guises. Whether they look old-fashioned, romantic, modern, or casual depends entirely on the vase you put them in, how you mix them with other flowers, and which colors you choose.*

## USING COLOR AND SHAPE

**COLOR SATURATION**
Float a yellow rose in a yellow glass container for dinner-party elegance.

**SYMPHONY IN WHITE**
A pillar candle and white roses sit well in a galvanized steel container.

**TEST-TUBE DISPLAY**
Stagger the height of the flowers for this modern look, and do not fill every tube.

STEMS cut at different heights make the display look casual

A FEW LEAVES add color contrast to the display

**"BOUDOIR" ROSES**
Cut strong pink roses low and balance them on the edge of a cream trophy vase, cramming their heads together.

LONGER STEMS and larger heads are positioned in the center of the arrangement

OUTER ROSES are arranged first, with their heads resting on the edge of the vase

METAL URN is not watertight, so it conceals a glass vase in which the roses are arranged

ENTRANCE-HALL DISPLAY
This classical metal urn calls for a classical mix of blooms. I have used slightly open, multicolored roses to give the impression of flowers just gathered from the garden.

# CARNATION POTS

TRY TO RESIST THE URGE to place a bunch of carnations in a vase: instead, take a few moments to transform these flowers by cutting them short and massing them together. Accept that they will never tumble daintily over the edge of a vase, and work instead with their major features: straight stems and candy colors. Here I have emphasized their characteristic hues by painting terracotta pots in complementary shades.

## MAKING THE DISPLAY

Use water-resistant oil paints to decorate the terracotta pots. It is an economical way to create vases in colors that will be suitable for your chosen flowers.

*1 Fill the tumbler with water and place it inside the terracotta pot.*

*2 Place the carnations in the glass, cutting the stems so the heads rest in a ring around the edge of the pot. To finish, fill the center with slightly longer stems.*

HEADS PACKED CLOSELY
together give dense color

TERRACOTTA POT painted
with water-resistant oil paint

**SEASONAL VARIATIONS**
Try using different colors
to match the seasons – red
flowers in a green pot for
Christmas, or orange flowers
in a brown pot for autumn.

# DIANTHUS DISPLAYS

CONTRARY TO POPULAR BELIEF, carnations can look
contemporary if you work with, rather than against,
their sugary colors. Bound together and placed in painted
terracotta pots, the long stems and full heads form
impressive topiary trees. A moody bouquet shows
off the drama of a dark variety, while a frothy lilac
arrangement brings sweet Williams, pinks, and
hydrangeas right up to date with a zingy painted pot.

BRIGHT RAFFIA
binds stems tightly
just below the heads

SUMPTUOUS RED
ROSES add an
extravagant touch

ROMANTIC BOUQUET
Make a posy (see page 114)
of stunning dark red carnations,
red roses, and sweet Williams.
Tie it with pink raffia.

## CARNATION TOPIARY TREES

The long, straight stems of
carnations are perfectly suited to
creating topiary trees. Add the
stems to your hand one by
one, bind tightly, and place in
a tumbler inside a painted pot.

CARNATION HEADS
are massed together
for an intense burst
of color

CARNATIONS and sweet
Williams fill gaps between
the hydrangea heads

## PURPLE VASE

Paint a pot with oil
paints in modern
colors that update the
old–fashioned look of
sweet Williams, pinks,
and hydrangeas.

# MODERN SUNFLOWERS

## — YOU WILL NEED —

*Cylindrical
glass vase*

*Large bundle
of raffia*

*5 large
sunflowers*

*10 small
sunflowers*

I HAVE USED BRIGHT YELLOW RAFFIA to magnify
the color of these bold sunflowers and give this
rustic look a modern twist. The height of the vase
balances out the bushiness of the flowerheads,
while the green foliage breaks up the yellow.
When the flowers start to wilt, pull the petals
off to reveal the green layer underneath, and use
different-colored raffia or upholstery cord for
a variation on the theme.

## MAKING THE DISPLAY

Cut the stems so they are slightly taller than the vase.
Leave the center ones slightly longer. To prevent rot,
strip off the leaves that will be below the water level.

*1 Starting at the bottom,
wind the raffia around
the vase. When you
come to the end of a
length of raffia, tie the
next length to it and
continue. Completely
cover the vase with raffia.*

*2 Fill the vase with
water. Place the
sunflowers in a ring
around the edge of
the vase, slanting the
stems so the heads rest
on the rim. To finish,
fill the center with
slightly longer stems,
and use any spare
leaves to fill gaps.*

SUNFLOWER LEAVES
add a contrasting
color to the display

RAFFIA hides the
clear glass vase,
giving it a brand-
new look

SUMMER SUN
Yellow raffia emphasizes the
sunny color of the flowers,
but gold cord would make a
creative alternative.

# SUNFLOWER DISPLAYS

WHEN USING SUNFLOWERS, it is too easy to let them take on their usual "country" look, so here I have used earthenware vases in warm colors to give the display a Provençal flair. In contrast, the three stems in modern glass tubes bring the arrangement up to date. When the petals start to wilt, try pulling them off to reveal the green underlayer. Do not be afraid to cut sunflowers down low – the single stem in the earthy, glazed pot is an example of how even a tight budget can achieve a stunning display. Sometimes less is definitely more.

**BRONZE AND GOLD**
Warm, sandy colors link these jaunty wooden blocks with the more traditional terracotta vases.

SUNFLOWERS with the petals removed provide a contrasting color

GLASS TUBES in wooden blocks add modern style

DECORATED TERRACOTTA
gives a Mediterranean look,
perfect for sunflowers

**SUNBURST**
Working from the outside
in, place the sunflowers in
concentric circles. Rest the
heads of the outer flowers
on the edge of the vase.

# FRUITY DAHLIAS

Vase     5 tangerines    9 dahlias with
on sticks      foliage

IF YOU WANT AN INNOVATIVE NEW LOOK, why limit yourself to flowers? For this fun–filled arrangement, I decided that vivid orange tangerines would make a perfect accompaniment for the wine–red pompon dahlias. The jaunty foliage stripped from the flowers breaks up the heavy colors and adds shape to the display, while a contemporary vase in tangy apricot emphasizes the dark petals of the dahlias.

## MAKING THE DISPLAY

Use scissors to make a hole in each tangerine. If they are strong enough, use the dahlia stems for sticks; otherwise, garden stakes or other woody stems will do.

*1 Fill the vase with water, then place the tangerines around the outer edge of the vase.*

*2 Add the dahlias between the fruit, filling gaps with foliage stripped from the flowers. To finish, place another ring of slightly taller dahlias and foliage in the center.*

CENTRAL DAHLIAS
are slightly taller
than the outer ones

FOLIAGE breaks up
the round shapes of the
flowers and tangerines

TANGERINES
supported on the rim
of the vase do not
squash the flowers

FRUIT AND FLOWERS
This arrangement
would also work using
apples, lemons, or limes
with matching flowers.

PLACE THE VASE on a low table
so it can be viewed from above.

# DAHLIA DISPLAYS

THE WIDE VARIETY OF COLORS, shapes, and sizes of dahlia makes it easy to create vibrant displays without introducing other types of flower. Here the lime-green plastic bowl reflects the almost artificial brightness of the blooms, giving a vivid, modern look to flowers more often seen in the garden. To make this arrangement, cut the dahlias down low and mass their heads together for an intense burst of late-summer color.

**SIMPLE BUT SWEET**
This display is proof that quantity is not everything. If you choose colors carefully, it is possible to make an impact without masses of flowers.

DARK RED DAHLIAS are set off by the lime-green bowl

CLUSTERS of same-color flowers give more impact than single blooms

LEAVES fill out the bowl

INNER BLOOMS have
slightly longer stems
than outer ones

**CLUSTERED FLOWERS**
Rest the heads of the outer circle
of flowers on the rim of the bowl.
Then work from the outside in,
resting each concentric circle on
the previous one.

DAHLIAS spill over
the side of the bowl

FOLIAGE frames
the flowers

# ORIENTAL LILIES

## YOU WILL NEED

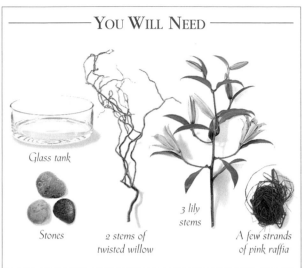

Glass tank

Stones

2 stems of
twisted willow

3 lily
stems

A few strands
of pink raffia

JUST A FEW LILY STEMS are needed to make this sculptured display, and look how it transforms the flowers! The look is modern and ethereal, hinting at Oriental style. The display's great height and elegance call for it to be placed on a side table in a large, but simple, room. I prefer to keep the flowers pale and use bright raffia to add flashes of color, but you could choose to highlight bold lilies with subtle raffia bows.

## MAKING THE DISPLAY

Prepare the display in position, since it is very heavy and awkward to lift once made. Change the water every few days.

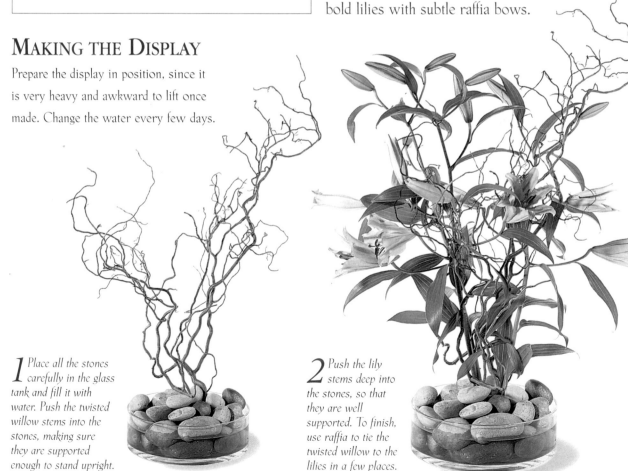

*1* Place all the stones carefully in the glass tank and fill it with water. Push the twisted willow stems into the stones, making sure they are supported enough to stand upright.

*2* Push the lily stems deep into the stones, so that they are well supported. To finish, use raffia to tie the twisted willow to the lilies in a few places.

RAFFIA BOWS
complement the
color of the lilies

STEMS are
supported by
the stones

WATER is deep enough
to reach the stems

## MINIMAL STYLE
This sparse arrangement suits
a house decorated in a minimal
style. It would look fantastic in
an uncluttered, airy room.

# LILY DISPLAYS

PURE AND ELEGANT, lilies demand simple containers to show them at their best. Heavy-bottomed clear glass vases are ideal: in a light room, where the sun catches the water, the effect is dazzling. Choose vases that mirror and complement the different shapes of the flowers – long calla lilies look best in a tall, thin vase, while a single white lily rests languidly on the rim of a low bowl.

DARK PINK
lilies clustered in
a square glass tank

FOLIAGE AND FLOWERS
drape over the edge of
the vase

**CRYSTAL CLEAR**
Enhance the sparkling effect of the glass vases by placing a few together, and change the water every day to keep it looking fresh and clean.

DARK GREEN monstera leaves highlight the pink of the Oriental lilies

CALLA LILIES call for a tall vase that supports the graceful stems

STEMS ARE STRIPPED of foliage to keep the water clean

# INSIDE-OUT GERBERAS

## YOU WILL NEED

Glass tumbler

Rubber band

Stems cut from 10 gerberas

Yellow string

10 gerberas

OFTEN THE PERFECT VASE is not at hand when you need it, so I believe in raiding the kitchen for equipment. These gerberas are arranged in an ordinary drinking glass that is hidden from view by a ring of crisp green stems tied in position with colored string. Two or three of these simple arrangements, using different-colored flowers, would look perfect on a window ledge or as a table centerpiece for a casual lunch party.

## MAKING THE DISPLAY

Cut the gerberas to the right height for the tumbler and save the stems for decoration. If the stems are not long enough to cover the tumbler, use green beans instead.

*1* Place a rubber band around the tumbler. Slide the cut stems under the band to encircle the tumbler completely.

*2* Bind the stems in position with yellow string, then remove the rubber band. Cut the circle of stems to the height of the tumbler, fill it with water, and arrange the flowers.

GERBERAS all cut to the same height convey the feeling of fullness

STRING tied in a simple knot adds charm and color contrast

THE "NO-VASE" SOLUTION
I first saw this method used by the Parisian florist, Christian Tortu. It works equally well with almost any long-stemmed flowers such as daffodils, anemones, and lachenalia.

# INSTANT EFFECTS WITH GERBERAS

*WHEN USING GERBERAS, it is important to match your flowers to the vases you have on hand. The myriad of colors available and the simple shape of the flowers mean a single stem can look stylish and modern, while abundant arrangements work well, too.*

## USING COLOR AND SHAPE

### DOUBLE STRENGTH
Keep vase and flowers the same color for maximum impact.

### TWO COLORS
Add a contrasting shade to bright yellow flowers with a yellow glass jar.

### LONG-STEMMED GERBERA
Use bright green glass to highlight the purity and freshness of this white flower.

### FIVE STEMS
Fill a narrow-necked vase with five stems that pick up the color of the vase.

### TEN STEMS
For a stronger arrangement, add five more stems in a complementary color.

### FIVE STEMS WITH FOLIAGE
One or two large leaves, such as these anthurium leaves, give instant drama.

FLOWERS at various
heights give the display
an informal look

GREEN STEMS without
foliage emphasize the
simplicity of the display

TERRACOTTA POT is not
watertight: it hides a glass jar in
which the gerberas are arranged

PERFECT PARTNERS
An ideal match of container and
flowers: the washed dots on the
terracotta reflect the pale color of the
gerberas, while the scalloped edge of
the pot echoes the shape of the petals.

# WATERMELON VASE

USING FRUIT TO MAKE A VASE gives the display originality. I have avoided filling this hollowed-out watermelon with a cocktail of tropical flowers, choosing instead to highlight the dusty gray-green tones of its skin with hydrangea and sea holly. Although too special for everyday use, this luscious arrangement could be a splendid feature at a buffet party, perhaps sitting alongside melons crammed with delicious finger food.

## MAKING THE DISPLAY

If you choose a large melon you will need more flowers and foliage to fill the shell.

1 *Slice the top off the watermelon and scoop out the flesh. Fill the shell with water, then place the ornamental cabbage at the front.*

2 *Add the hydrangea and ivy to the arrangement, working around the edge of the melon shell. To finish, place the sea holly in the center.*

BLUE SEA HOLLY picks out the blue tones of the cabbage leaves

THICK GREEN LEAVES of the ornamental cabbage make a dramatic centerpiece for the display

**CHANGING SEASONS**
To adapt the look to suit the changing seasons, you could also use pumpkins, gourds, squash, and cabbages.

# IVY WREATHS

| | | | |
|---|---|---|---|
| *5 twiggy branches* | *5 branches of twigs, sprayed gold* | *String*<br>*3 long strands of ivy, lightly gilded with gold spray paint* | *3½ yd (3m) of rope, sprayed gold* |

THE TRADITIONAL APPROACH to wreathmaking requires time, patience, specialized equipment, and expertise, but these simple wreaths, made from winter foliage, prove that original and modern looks can be achieved in a few minutes. The method adapts well to different styles – holly branches give the wreath a truly Christmassy feel, but bare twigs could be decorated with foliage and scented flowers for summer.

## MAKING AN IVY WREATH

Choose only the freshest, most supple twigs and branches to make this wreath, or it will be difficult to bend them into a circle. Use gold spray paint to highlight leaves and branches for a more opulent effect.

*1* One by one, twist the branches around each other to form a long, thick piece, binding with string if necessary. Bend into a circle and bind tightly. Form the wreath into shape, and snip off messy pieces to fill gaps.

*2* Wind the ivy in and around the wreath, positioning the gold leaves evenly throughout. To finish, cover the string by winding the gold rope around it, leaving a decorative strand of rope hanging down each side of the wreath.

GOLD ROPE is left hanging
to give the wreath a
contemporary elegance

### FESTIVE FOLIAGE
The type of foliage you choose
has a direct impact on the final look
of the wreath. For a traditional
Christmas look (above), team fresh
branches of berried holly with a
luxurious shot–silk ribbon in rich
tones of red and green.

# SPRING ARRANGEMENTS

SPRING FLOWERS need minimum fuss for maximum impact. The secret is to choose a vessel that works with the flowers and the interior of your house, but remember that the vase can dramatically alter the mood of a display. I have picked orange containers to exaggerate the hues of the lachenalia and fritillaria, while galvanized buckets give a more contemporary feel, particularly when arranged in a line and teamed with flowers in glorious shades.

**ALL IN A ROW**
Blue muscari, green ivy, and bright primroses in miniature galvanized buckets create cheerful bursts of color.

SILVERY SENECIO reflects the tone of the container

**SPRING COLORS**
To create a group
of arrangements
that work well
together, balance
heights and colors
when you choose
the containers.

**FIERY PITCHER** picks
up the warm hues of
the fritillaria

**LACHENALIA** drapes
gently over the side
of a coffee mug

# SUMMER ARRANGEMENT

MASSES OF SUMMER FLOWERS are packed into this enamel tub to
create a natural-looking display of summer abundance in the
countryside. Although the flowers are placed randomly
in the tub, they are grouped together by
type, as if they were still growing in
the garden. It is a versatile look that
works with many types of flower;
try mixing size and color to
achieve the look you want.

YELLOW CALENDULAS
add color between the
pink peonies and green
lady's mantle

WHITE PLUMELIKE
astilbe contrasts with the
lushness of peonies

WHITE ASTRANTIA
softens the clash of deep
blue cornflowers and
vivid orange calendulas

GARDEN BOUNTY
Group each type of flower into
a bunch, bind them, and cut the
stems flat. Fill the tub with
enough water to cover the
stems, then position the flowers.

# AUTUMN ARRANGEMENT

THIS BOUNTIFUL DISPLAY OF BERRIES and fruit crammed into
an earthy terracotta pot reflects the abundance of the
autumn harvest. The wide-necked container
gives the display a full, rounded shape,
allowing the components to drape
decadently over the sides.

AUTUMNAL EUCALYPTUS
contrasts with red of rosehips

FRESH APPLES are speared
on sticks, then positioned

TERRACOTTA POT is the
quintessential container
for autumnal arrangements

PURPLE SMOKETREE
contrasts with other
autumn colors

BERRIED IVY is a
patch of green between
hypericum berries
and euonymus berries

HYDRANGEA flowers
are positioned with
heads hanging down
to look natural

HARVEST FESTIVAL
Place bundles of foliage
in a bucket inside the
terracotta pot, putting
the taller bundles at the
back and pointing bunches
in different directions.

# WINTER ARRANGEMENTS

THESE SEASONAL DISPLAYS demonstrate the importance of coordinating vase color with content. A vase can exaggerate and emphasize tones and shades, dramatically changing the impact of the flowers. Below, I have dusted variegated ivy with a hint of silver paint to reflect the frosted feel of the cast-iron container while, on the right, I have matched bright red berries and dark foliage with a red glass vase for festive winter warmth.

PROMINENT LEAVES are highlighted with a hint of silver spray paint

CAST-IRON CONTAINER enhances the pale, frosted tones of the flowers and foliage

**SILVER AND WHITE**
Randomly mass together hyacinths, ranunculus, Christmas roses, mistletoe, eucalyptus, and variegated ivy dusted with silver paint.

VASE looks striking
when light shines
through the red glass

BERRY RED
A mixture of dark winter
foliage and berries goes
perfectly with a deep red
glass vase: in another
container the effect would
be less dramatic.

# SPECIAL EFFECTS

PARTIES AND SPECIAL OCCASIONS CALL FOR MORE THAN JUST A BUNCH

OF BLOOMS ON A SHELF OR WINDOWSILL – THEY PROVIDE THE PERFECT

EXCUSE FOR ADORNING YOUR HOME WITH CREATIVE COMBINATIONS OF

VIVID FLOWERS, VIBRANT GREEN FOLIAGE, AND MELLOW CANDLELIGHT.

OFTEN THE FOCAL POINT OF A ROOM, MANTELPIECES CAN SERVE AS

CENTER STAGE FOR A CELEBRATION, WHILE A FEW SIMPLE FLOWERS AND

SOME TRAILING FOLIAGE ON A DINING TABLE CAN EFFECT A MAGICAL

TRANSFORMATION FOR AN EVENING PARTY.

THE PAGES THAT FOLLOW FEATURE A SELECTION OF MY FAVORITE

IDEAS FOR YOU TO ADAPT TO SUIT YOUR PERSONAL STYLE.

# SUMMER TABLE DISPLAY

## YOU WILL NEED

15 stems of
dark ivy

Petals from 2
striped roses

26
striped
roses

WHEN TIME IS OF THE ESSENCE, a table setting
can be swiftly transformed by weaving trails of
ivy and dappled rose heads among the plates,
then scattering the display with fragrant rose
petals. Napkins wound with a piece of ivy
and a single rose complete the romantic
summer table. Deep red roses combine
equally well with ivy for a sumptuous
Christmas display.

## MAKING THE DISPLAY

Trail ivy all around and over the edge of the table.
Place rose heads in clusters on the table and tuck rose
leaves beneath them, then sprinkle petals on
the tablecloth.

A SPRIG OF LEAVES lies
beneath the cut–down
rose stem

*1 Tie a length of ivy loosely around a
rolled napkin. Trim the ivy, making sure
the ends are long enough to trail over the
rim of a side plate.*

*2 Cut down a rose stem to about 4in
(10cm) and remove the leaves. Tuck
a sprig of leaves under the twist
of ivy, then push in the rose.*

TRAILS OF IVY create
long, flowing lines

# PACIFIC-STYLE TABLE

Pink
string

4 ginger
flowers

2 ginger
leaves

2 anthurium
leaves

BRING A SUGGESTION OF THE ORIENT to your dining room with this exotic table setting, which is based on clever use of striking colors. Set against an azure tablecloth, the lustrous pink flowers and dark, glossy leaves are fast and easy to arrange yet sophisticated enough to impress even the most discerning dinner guests.

## MAKING THE DISPLAY

Make sure the ginger leaves are supple enough to bend around the flower stems – if they are too dry they will crack.

FIVE PIECES OF STRING tied in one knot add decorative detail

**1** Strip any foliage from the ginger flowers and place two stems together. Wrap a ginger leaf around the stems.

**2** Cut five lengths of pink string and use them all to tie the wrapped leaf in place. To finish, place in the center of the table, on top of the anthurium leaves.

# CHRISTMAS DINING TABLE

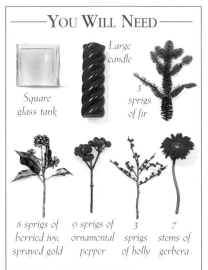

### — YOU WILL NEED —

Square glass tank

Large candle

3 sprigs of fir

8 sprigs of berried ivy, sprayed gold

9 sprigs of ornamental pepper

3 sprigs of holly

7 stems of gerbera

NO CHRISTMAS TABLE is complete without candles and flowers, yet who wants to spend the festive season hunting for specialized equipment? This simple candle and foliage display is quickly assembled and can be prepared at the last minute or a few days in advance. If you cannot find gerberas, choose other bold flowers in colors to complement your tableware.

## MAKING THE DISPLAY

If you have time, expand the theme by laying a single bloom on each napkin and tying a name tag to each flower.

*1* Place the candle in the center of the glass tank, then fill the tank with water. Position the fir sprigs around the candle, pointing them in different directions.

*2* Add the berried ivy, ornamental peppers, and holly around the candle. Dot the gerberas around the center to finish.

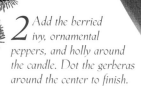

# BEACHCOMBER MANTELPIECE

BLUES, GREENS, AND GRAYS, pebbles and rope: these bits and pieces look as if they have been gradually gathered from a blustery seaside and placed lovingly on this mantelpiece. Standing in simple glass tumblers, eucalyptus and cabbage continue the natural theme, while a hand–tied bundle of eucalyptus pods is propped casually behind the stone candle holders.

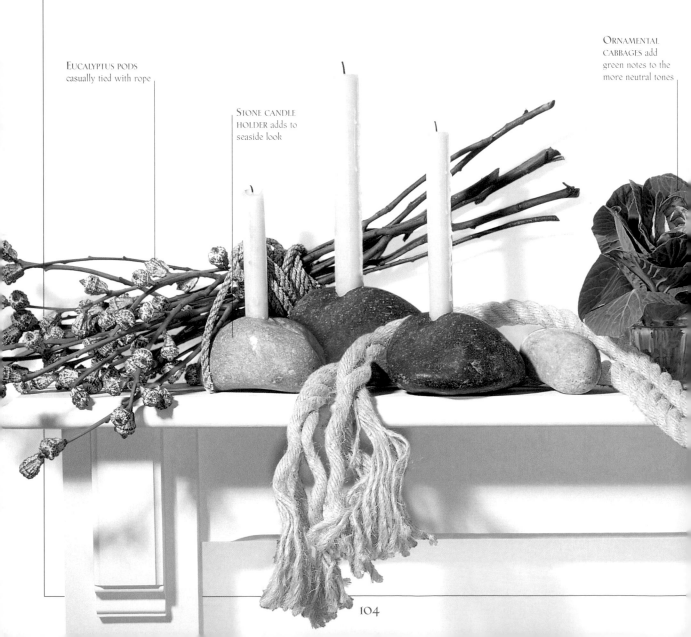

ORNAMENTAL CABBAGES add green notes to the more neutral tones

EUCALYPTUS PODS casually tied with rope

STONE CANDLE HOLDER adds to seaside look

SILVER-GRAY TONES
of the eucalyptus pods add
to the beachcomber image

PEBBLES enhance
the colors of the
cabbages and
eucalyptus pods

ROPE ties the
display together

# GERBERA MANTELPIECE

THE KEY TO THIS DISPLAY is its simplicity. Clear glass containers allow the long, curvy gerbera stems to become as much a feature of the display as the blooms, while the jelly-bean colors of these modest flowers make them a winning choice for a contemporary interior. Fewer stems, rather than more, will keep the look uncluttered and bold. Other flowers with strong colors, large heads, and bare stems, such as tulips, anemones, and amaryllis, work in similar arrangements.

DIFFERENT AMOUNTS of water in each vase create an interesting visual effect

GERBERA stems are cut
to varying lengths to give
an idea of spontaneity

LONG, BENDY STEMS
are a feature
of the display

### TWO OR TEN
This display is just as striking
if you use only a few containers.

# ANEMONE MANTELPIECE

REPETITION AND REGULARITY lie at the heart of this graphic arrangement: the anemones are equidistant, and each laurel leaf hangs at exactly the same height. Wrap laurel leaves around glass tumblers and tie with wire, then fill the glasses with anemones, packing their heads together. Suspend extra laurel leaves from lengths of wire.

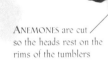

GLOSSY LEAVES
are hung at exactly
the same height

ANEMONES are cut
so the heads rest on the
rims of the tumblers

LAUREL LEAVES
wrapped around
the tumbler

### SUSPENDING LEAVES
Twist the wire around the stem of each leaf, then hang the leaves above the mantelpiece.

### ALTERNATIVE IDEA
If you cannot find laurel leaves, try making the display with fresh ivy leaves.

GOLDEN WIRE ties the wrapped leaves in place

# GREEN CANDELABRA

## YOU WILL NEED

*Candelabra*

*15 baby's tears in 3 shades of green*

*6 candles*

*1 large glass jar*

*16 glass jars*

*2 glass vases*

IF YOU THINK A CANDELABRA is too elaborate for everyday use, try dressing it down with plants such as these delicate green baby's tears. I have used lime candles and green glass to emphasize the radiant color of the leaves and to contrast with the hard silver color of the metal. Use the candelabra as a dining table centerpiece, or remove the inner ring of plants, light the candles, and hang it from the ceiling instead.

## MAKING THE DISPLAY

Introduce more color by filling some of the pots with cut flowers or candles in different shades.

*1 Place the candelabra in position on the table. Remove the baby's tears from their pots and replant in the small glass jars. Place the plants in a few of the candelabra holders and in a ring around the inside of the candelabra.*

*2 Fill the remaining candelabra holders with plants and candles in jars and vases. To finish, put three candles in the large glass jar, then place it in the center of the ring.*

HOOK allows candelabra to hang if the arrangement is adapted accordingly

GLOW IN THE DARK
If you wish to use the candelabra at night, replace a few plants with extra candles to give more light.

CLUSTER OF CANDLES draws the eye to the center of the candelabra

INNER RING of plants gives the impression of fullness

# GIFT IDEAS

FLOWERS CAN MAKE A SUPERB LAST-MINUTE GIFT. IT TAKES JUST

A FEW FRESH IDEAS TO TURN A MODEST BUNCH OF FLOWERS

INTO A BEAUTIFUL BOUQUET OR GIFT

ARRANGEMENT. SOME OF THE FOLLOWING

SUGGESTIONS REQUIRE A LITTLE ADVANCE

PLANNING, BUT, FOR THOSE OF YOU WANTING INSTANT

RESULTS, I HAVE INCLUDED IDEAS THAT WILL ENABLE

YOU TO TURN EVEN A HASTILY PREPARED GIFT INTO

A MINIATURE MASTERPIECE OF SIMPLE DESIGN.

# BRIDAL POSY

## YOU WILL NEED

50 stems
of freesia

Twine

White tulle, 3¼ x 1 yd
(3 x 1m)

THE SWEET PERFUME OF FREESIAS makes them a perpetual favorite with brides. Update the candy-colored freesia posy of the sixties by keeping to a single-color bunch and using large-headed double freesias. This extravagant posy of luscious, creamy flowers becomes quite ethereal when swathed in masses of white tulle; white ribbon tied in a bow would give a more understated look, yet still be effective.

## MAKING THE POSY

For an opulent look, choose luxurious double freesias. Bind the stems tightly so the posy does not fall apart during the day.

STEMS placed at
an angle make a
spiral shape

*1 Hold one stem in your hand, then build up the posy by adding stems one by one, each stem at slightly more of an angle than the last.*

*2 Use twine to bind the flowers tightly just below the heads. Cut the stems level and to a length that is comfortable to hold in the hand.*

**3** Cut a strip of tulle 12in x 1yd (30cm x 1m). Fold the remaining tulle in half lengthwise and scrunch it up in both hands. Wrap it around the posy so the stems are covered. Use the cut strip to tie the tulle in place.

**PERFECT POSY**
The white freesias and tulle make this ideal for a bride; use brighter flowers and a different fabric for a bridesmaid.

# Bold Bouquets

WITH A LITTLE IMAGINATION, bouquets can be made to suit practically any person and almost every situation, as these flamboyant and contemporary examples show. Swathes of ruffled tissue paper make the bouquets themselves look like huge exotic flowers – choose colors to complement or contrast with the blooms. Use the method for making posies on page 114.

CRIMSON PAPER complements inky purple monkshoods, pink roses, calla lilies, eucalyptus, and dark green foliage

CERISE TISSUE PAPER
encircles frothy hydrangeas
and lush roses in pink and red

GREEN CHRYSANTHEMUMS,
poppy heads, variegated
boxwood, sedum, and *Garrya
elliptica* are arranged around
anthuriums and wrapped in
lime-colored tissue paper

GIFT-WRAPPED BOUQUET
For an extra-special wrapping
(see above), hold the flowers
upright in the center of a
square of tissue paper.
Gather the paper up
around the stems
and tie just below
the heads.

# PLANTED ORCHIDS

4 potted
phalaenopsis
orchids

Wooden trug lined
with plastic

Selection
of shells
and pebbles

2 terracotta
pots

A few handfuls
of sand

3 handfuls
of moss

4 shells
on raffia

A REALLY SPECIAL GIFT, these plants outshine cut flowers every time. Always consider the recipient's surroundings and personality when making a gift, and look carefully at the flowers for help choosing a container. The bleached colors and tropical blooms in this arrangement would suit a modern, airy environment; the size of the trug and height of the flowers make it ideal for a low table.

## MAKING THE DISPLAY

Take the orchids out of the arrangement to water them; the display should last 4 weeks or more.

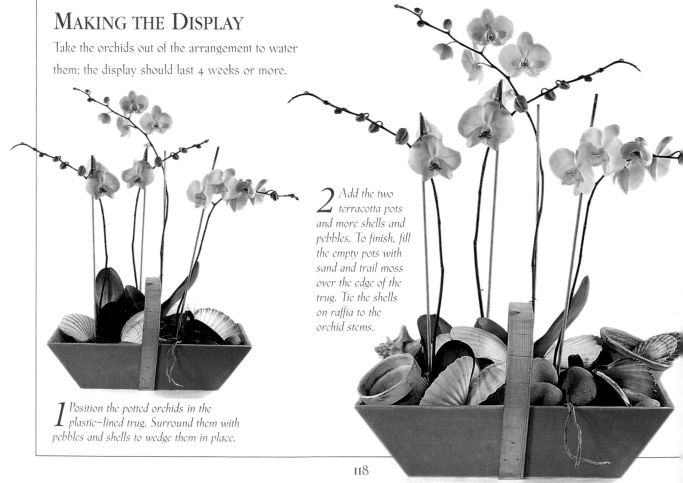

**2** Add the two terracotta pots and more shells and pebbles. To finish, fill the empty pots with sand and trail moss over the edge of the trug. Tie the shells on raffia to the orchid stems.

**1** Position the potted orchids in the plastic-lined trug. Surround them with pebbles and shells to wedge them in place.

**IDEAL GIFT**
This effective display
is surprisingly easy
to assemble and evokes
thoughts of sunny days.

RAFFIA is
decorated
with shells

ORCHID ROOTS
dangle over the
edge of the trug

# VALENTINE HEART

8 dark red roses

6 pink roses

8 stems of fuchsia

4 stems of photinia

4 stems of hypericum

Gold string

2¼ x 2¼yd (2 x 2m) of cellophane

Red tissue paper

Heart-shaped box

WHY NOT CELEBRATE VALENTINE'S DAY with a posy made from roses, the emblem of romance? This lush explosion of velvety pink and berry red fits snugly into a heart-shaped box to make a glamorous surprise for your loved one. Although roses are particularly sensitive to water deprivation, the cellophane wrapping holds enough water to sustain them until they can be transferred to a vase.

## MAKING THE POSY

Cut the stems to a length that matches the depth of the box, allowing the lid to fit comfortably without damaging the heads of the flowers.

*1 Make the posy (see page 114). Measure out enough cellophane to gather up around it and create a "pouch." Place the posy in the center of the cellophane.*

*2 Gather the cellophane around the posy and tie it carefully with string. Fill the bottom of the cellophane pouch with water by pouring it down through the middle of the posy. To finish, place the posy upright in the box.*

PHOTINIA adds lightness
to the display while
continuing the red theme

A SINGLE ROSE
is tied to the lid
with gold cord

RED TISSUE PAPER
lining the box adds
drama to this
sumptuous gift

VALENTINE GLAMOUR
The different tones of
red and the delicate pink
fuchsia give the impression
of opulence and, ultimately,
of romance.

# WRAPPING GIFTS

BEFORE YOU REACH FOR BOWS AND RIBBONS, look how a well-chosen flower can transform an ordinary package. A silver box with two *Amaryllis belladonna* attached could contain an anniversary present, while the same box adorned with a single, triffidlike anthurium promises something exotic. Try raiding the garden for material: a hydrangea and some string can look frivolous yet fresh where a bow might look fussy.

PUFFY PINK HYDRANGEA is an attractive alternative to a bow

PINK RIBBON intertwined with *Amaryllis belladonna* adds feminine charm

A PEACH-COLORED GERBERA complements a lilac bag

**BAGS OF STYLE**
Floral decorations are an easy way to personalize gifts, instantly giving them a homemade look.

PURPLE PUFFBALL ALLIUMS peek out of a gift bag

AN ANTHURIUM jazzes up a striped ribbon

A SIMPLE CALLA LILY adds elegance to a long, gold box

A LEUCOSPERMUM tied with yellow string hints at the exotic

# TECHNIQUES & SKILLS

ANY FLOWER ARRANGEMENT, whatever the size, will last longer if you take a couple of minutes to prepare the stems in advance. The basic techniques on these pages show how to spiral stems to give your displays a good shape, and how to cut and clean stems to encourage flowers to take up water. A method for straightening stems is also included: this can strengthen flowers as well as make them look more healthy.

## SPIRALING STEMS

*1 Hold the first stem in one hand, then add the next at a diagonal angle. One by one, add more stems, each one at slightly more of an angle than the previous one.*

*2 Continue adding the stems in this manner to form a spiral pattern. Use your thumb to hold them in position.*

*3 When the bunch is complete, cut the stems to the same length and drop them into the vase, letting them fall naturally into shape.*

# PREPARING STEMS

 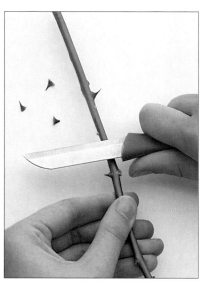 

*1* Strip the stems of all foliage that will be below the waterline. This helps keep the water clean and looks neat and tidy.

*2* Gently scrape each stem with a knife. This removes any thorns, bumps, and old plant tissue from the stems.

*3* Cut the stems on a slant. This creates a larger surface area, which allows the stem to take up water more efficiently.

# STRAIGHTENING STEMS

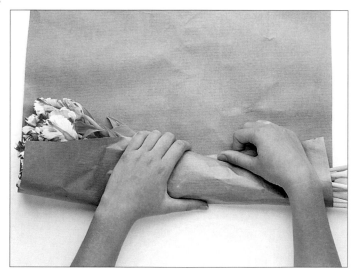 

*1* Straight flower stems give an arrangement extra height and make flowers that tend to wilt quickly, such as tulips, easier to display. To straighten bent stems, wrap them in brown paper and secure with tape or string.

*2* Stand the wrapped stems in a deep container of warm, fresh water for a few hours, or overnight, until they straighten.

# INDEX

## Author's Acknowledgments

I would like to say a big thank you to my wonderful team
at my shops and school for all their help and support.

Thank you, too, to Annabel, Emy, and Tracey for endless diligence
and help in producing this book and for always pushing things a
little further. A huge thank you to Dave King for his wonderful
photography, patience, and help, and grateful thanks to June for those
fantastic lunches that saw us all through.

## Publisher's Acknowledgments

Dorling Kindersley would like to thank Claudia Norris and
Rachana Devidayal for design assistance; Nasim Mawji, Lorna
Damms, Monica Chakraverty, and David Summers for editorial
assistance; Stephen Einhorn for the stone candle holders on pages
104–5; Tony Cross and Pam Brinkhurst at Wilford Bulb Company;
Philip Tivey & Sons, growers of dahlias and other plants since
1956; John Mattock; David Root at Kelways Ltd; Langport, Somerset;
Bloms Bulbs Ltd, Bedford; the Flower Council of Holland.
Photography by Dave King except: Mark Hamilton 35, 94–5.
Index: Sue Bosanko